TEACHING ENGLISH

Around the World

Creation Lessons for Short-Term Mission Trips

Cheryl B. Parker

CROSSBOOKS
PUBLISHING

CrossBooks™
A Division of LifeWay
1663 Liberty Drive
Bloomington, IN 47403
www.crossbooks.com
Phone: 1-866-879-0502

First published by CrossBooks 3/26/2011

ISBN: 978-1-6150-7784-7 (sc)

Library of Congress Control Number: 2011925246

Printed in the United States of America

This book is printed on acid-free paper.

Acknowledgments

I am thankful to all the people who helped me develop these lessons. I never would have thought about the need for this book had it not been for the ministry of my friend Wanda Iliff and her husband Mike. Their organization, Asian Athletic Institute, opened the doors for us to be able to minister in a school in Thailand. Their invitation to join them in their ministry and teach English was the beginning of my search for an effective curriculum, which led me to develop these lessons. Thank you, Wanda and Mike, for your heart for people, for your ministry, and for your friendship throughout the years.

I am grateful to the members of the first team that used these lessons when they were still rough drafts; I applaud and thank them for their resourcefulness and flexibility as we used these lessons and adapted them to our situation.

My sister Nancy Smith and my friend Marilyn Dalton , both experienced school teachers, were both instrumental in the development of these lessons and activities. I couldn't have done it without you!

My thanks also go to friends at Operation Mobilization for their encouragement and suggestions when I decided to step out in faith and publish these lessons. Mark Vander Hoven helped me hone the title to enhance the book's effectiveness, and Heather Laba not only encouraged me to continue with this project but also read and made constructive suggestions for improving its content. Thank you both!

And thanks to my cousin, Rob Barge, of Hardware Graphic Design & Illustration, for putting his time and talents into the cover design of this book.

Lastly, thanks go to my husband, Steve Parker, for his constant encouragement not only for the publication of this book but also throughout the last forty years of marriage. I love you. Thank you for all that you have done to help me bring this book to print.

My prayer is that God will use the efforts of all that contributed to this book to change lives and bring glory to Him.

Introduction

I am not a teacher. I designed this curriculum out of necessity and was successful only because God took my desire and led me step-by-step.

In 2005, I reconnected with a childhood friend. Wanda and her husband Mike were missionaries in Southeast Asia and invited my husband and me to organize a trip from our church and help them in their ministry. I wanted to go but felt totally inadequate to contribute anything. What could I do? Their ministry was sports-based. They would typically use athletes to help coach, build sports programs, and establish friendships, with the ultimate goal of telling participants about God's love and His redemptive plan for their lives. They suggested that our team could teach English to high school students at the orphanage/school where they were working. I agreed and then was immediately overwhelmed by the responsibility. Even though I had attended a course at my church to learn to teach English as a second language (ESL), I knew that the information I had learned would not provide all that I needed to prepare for this trip. And so the adventure in developing this curriculum began!

I began to explore ideas for teaching English with the class time limited to only a week. How could we make the most impact when our time with the students would be only days instead of months? A trip to a Christian bookstore with a friend inspired me to develop each lesson around a day of creation. Each person I talked with contributed ideas. As we worked, God pulled it all together into a usable format.

Flexibility is a crucial component of any mission trip. We discovered that our trip to Southeast Asia was no different! Fortunately, the lessons included in this curriculum can be modified easily to meet various specific situations. We had planned to teach one lesson per day to several different classes. However, when we arrived at the school we were told that we would have one class all day long each day! We adjusted our plans easily, and you can do the same. The lessons presented here can be used in whole or in part. You can pick and choose according to your need.

These lessons do not follow traditional ESL principles. For instance, there is much more vocabulary than would really be possible for a non-English speaking person to learn in only a week or two. They are not intended to be a course in English in and of themselves. The goal is evangelism, and the lessons point to that purpose. Each lesson provides opportunities for the team to interact with their group of students. Some individuals in the class may have more English background than others. That's okay. Whether a student retains a little or a lot, our goal remains the same. We have found that even if a student has studied English in school and can speak it well, she will look forward to being able to practice her English skills with a native English speaker. The student who knows very little English or no English will come away with some basic vocabulary but will not be able to retain all that is taught in these lessons. These lessons can all be used very effectively in spite of the varied skill levels present in the classroom.

Another non-traditional aspect of this curriculum is the recommended use of a translator. A translator is crucial for a short-term team since the amount of time the team will spend with the class is limited. There is not time to fully incorporate ESL principles without the use of a translator.

We used previous drafts of these lessons several more times since our initial endeavor. Each time the team was successful in not only teaching English, but also in establishing a relationship with the students and leading many to come to know the Lord as their personal Savior. It is my hope and prayer that these formalized, published lessons will be used many more times as a tool to impact the world for Christ.

Each lesson is divided into the following segments:
- Theme
- Materials Needed
- Objectives
- Introduction
- Activities
- Optional Activity: Teaching Idioms
- Conclusion

Each activity will involve introducing vocabulary, a dialogue demonstrated by two teachers using the vocabulary, class repetition using the vocabulary, and a drill to reinforce the vocabulary.

The lessons are written in a bullet point format. These bullet points serve as talking points for your class.

There are several suggested activities for each lesson. Choose the one or ones that best meet your need and situation. Not all will work for each group.

Obtain all materials, if possible, prior to the trip. We depended on the school to provide the dry-erase board or chalkboard. In the event that a dry-erase board or chalkboard is not available, poster board with markers or a flip chart will work just as well. This is something that you should investigate prior to your trip and plan accordingly. We packed the flannel cloth in our suitcases; however, we bought a large piece of cardboard once we arrived and pinned the cloth to the board to use in front of the class. We were able to buy the felt creation story, the world beach ball and the EvangeCube˚ at a local Christian bookstore. Each lesson itemizes the materials needed, and a master list of all the materials needed for all the lessons is in the appendix. To encourage participation, we offered candy and other small items as rewards to the students. Pencils, pens, stickers, and small toys are all items that you can use as rewards. In many locations, students treasure these items, which are difficult to obtain in certain parts of the world.

Let's get started! Have fun!

English Lesson One

Theme: Creation, Day One—*"In the beginning..."*

Materials Needed

- World map
- Flannel cloth and board
- Felt "creation" story with piece of black flannel
- "World" beach ball
- Chalk and eraser or dry-erase markers
- Candy, stickers, small toys, pens, and/or pencils
- 8½-by-11-inch card stock to write Bible verse words
- Black marker

Objectives

At the end of lesson one, students will:

- Demonstrate an understanding of the vocabulary words in this lesson.
- Be able to repeat and understand the dialogues.
- Repeat the memory verse: "In the beginning, God created the heavens and the earth" (Genesis 1:1).
- Discuss what God did on the first day of creation.

Introduction

Start the class with introductions of your team. One team member can then take charge of the class and through the translator lead the following discussion points.

I was amazed at the response that we received when we asked the following first question to the class of teenagers. Their response was overwhelming and enthusiastic! Wanting to know where we came from is a universal, deep-seated desire that God has placed in all people everywhere. This was evident as we started our class. The students were immediately interested, and the topic held their attention for the entire class time! Use the following as a guide for talking with the class:

- Have you ever wondered where you came from?
- God's book, the Bible, gives us the answer to that question.
- The first book of the Bible, Genesis, means *the beginning*.
- Here we will find the answer to all beginnings.
- This week we are going to explore the beginning and how God made the world. We will have seven lessons and talk each day about what God did on that day. He made the whole world in seven days, so at the end of our lessons, you will know how God made the world.
- Each day we will also practice English by learning new words and how to put these words into correct English sentences.
- Today, since we are talking about beginnings, we will look at introductions and how we meet and greet people. We are new to you, and you are new to us. We'll start with learning each other's names.

A translator is crucial in order to teach these lessons.
Photo by Steve Parker

Activity One—Hello

Vocabulary for Activity One
- Hello
- Meet
- Name
- Meeting
- Is
- My
- You
- I'm
- Too

Dialogue for Activity One

A. "Hello. My name is _____."
B. "Hi. I'm _____. Nice to meet you."
A. "Nice meeting you, too."

1. **Introduce Vocabulary**
   - Write the words on the board.
   - Review the words with the students.

2. **Model/Comprehension Check**
   - Teacher A: "Hello. My name is _____"
   - Teacher B: "Hi. I'm _____. Nice to meet you."
   - Teacher A: "Nice to meet you too."

3. **Repetition of Dialogue between Teacher and Group**
   - Teacher: "Hello. My name is _____."
   - Group: "Hello. My name is _____."
   - Teacher: "Hi. I'm _____. Nice to meet you."
   - Group: "Hi. I'm _____. Nice to meet you."
   - Teacher: "Nice meeting you too."
   - Group: "Nice meeting you too."

Repetition with Response

- Teacher: "Hello. My name is _____."
- Group: "Hi. I'm _____. Nice to meet you."
- Teacher: "Nice to meet you too."

4. **Drill**

- Have students form two lines facing each other.
- Using the "world" beach ball, have a student introduce himself and then throw ball to another student for response, and then repeat until everyone has a chance.

Activity Two—How Are You?

Vocabulary for Activity Two
- How
- Are
- Fine
- Thank
- Thanks
- Just
- Good
- Morning
- Afternoon
- Evening

Dialogue for Activity Two

A. "Hello (or Good Morning, Good Afternoon, or Good Evening). How are you?"

B. "Fine, thank you. And you?"

A. "Just fine, thanks."

1. **Introduce Vocabulary**

- Write the words on the board.
- Review the words with the students.

2. Model/Comprehension Check

- Teacher A: "Hello (or Good Morning, Good Afternoon, or Good Evening). How are you?"
- Teacher B: "Fine, thank you. And you?"
- Teacher A: "Just fine, thanks."

3. Repetition of Dialogue between Teacher and Group

- Teacher: "Hello. How are you?"
- Group: "Hello. How are you?"
- Teacher: "Fine, thank you. And you?"
- Group: "Fine, thank you. And you?"
- Teacher: "Just fine, thanks."
- Group: "Just fine, thanks."

Repetition with Response

- Teacher: "Hello. How are you?"
- Group: "Fine, thank you. And you?"
- Teacher: "Just fine, thanks."

4. Drill

- Divide the class into three or more groups. (Have one teacher for each group.)
- Have two student volunteers come to the front and practice dialogue with each other. (Give candy to each participant after practice.)

Activity Three—Introductions

Vocabulary for Activity Three

- Hi
- I'd (I would)
- Like
- To
- Introduce
- Friend
- Brother
- Sister
- Mother
- Father
- Husband
- Wife

Dialogue for Activity Three

A. "Hi! How are you?"
B. "Fine. And you?"
A. "Fine, thanks. I'd like to introduce you to my friend, _____."
C. "Nice to meet you."

1. **Introduce Vocabulary**

   - Write the words on the board.
   - Review the words with the students.

2. **Model/Comprehension Check**

   Teacher A: "Hi! How are you?"
   Teacher B: "Fine. And you?"
   Teacher A: "Fine, thanks. I'd like to introduce you to my friend, _____."
   Teacher C: "Nice to meet you."

3. **Repetition of Dialogue between Teacher and Group**

   - Teacher: "Hi! How are you?"
   - Group: "Hi! How are you?"
   - Teacher: "Fine. And you?"

- Group: "Fine. And you?"
- Teacher: "Fine, thanks. I'd like to introduce you to my friend, _____."
- Group: "Fine, thanks. I'd like to introduce you to my friend, _____."

Repetition with Response

- Teacher: "Hi! How are you?"
- Group: "Fine. And you?"
- Teacher: "Fine, thanks. I'd like to introduce you to my friend, _____."

4. **Drill: "Pass It On" Activity**

- Make a large circle or several small circles.
- First Student: "Hi! How are you?"
- Second Student: "Fine. And you?"
- First Student: "Fine, thanks. I'd like to introduce you to my friend, _____ (third student's name)."
- Repeat, starting with the second student.

Activity Four—Where Are You From?

> *Vocabulary for Activity Four*
> - And
> - From
> - America

Dialogue for Activity Four

A. "Hi, my name is _____, and I'm from _____."

1. **Introduce Vocabulary**

- Write the words on the board.
- Review the words with the students.

2. **Model/Comprehension Check**
   - Teacher A: "Hi, my name is _____, and I'm from _____."
   - Teacher B: "Hi, my name is _____, and I'm from _____."

3. **Repetition of Dialogue between Teacher and Group**
   - Teacher: "Hi, my name is _____, and I'm from _____."
   - Group: "Hi, my name is _____, and I'm from _____."

4. **Drill**
   - Divide the students into small groups with a teacher in each group.
   - Work with each student individually in the group to repeat the dialogue.
   - If students are from different cities or localities in the area, you can also have them practice with each other.

Activity Five—Connect Today's Lesson to the First Day of Creation

Dialogue for Activity Five

"In the beginning God created the heavens and the earth" (Genesis 1:1).

Vocabulary for Activity Five
• In
• The
• Beginning
• God
• Created
• Heavens
• Earth

1. **Introduce Vocabulary**
   - Write the words on the board.
   - Review the words with the students.

2. **Model/Comprehension Check**
   - Teacher A: "In the beginning God created the heavens and the earth." (Genesis 1:1)
   - Teacher B: "In the beginning God created the heavens and the earth." (Genesis 1:1)

3. **Repetition of Dialogue between Teacher and Group**
   - Teacher: "In the beginning God created the heavens and the earth" (Genesis 1:1).
   - Group: "In the beginning God created the heavens and the earth" (Genesis 1:1).

4. **Drill**
   - Select ten students to come to the front of room. Give each one a poster of one of the ten words.
   - Mix them up and have students put themselves in order (if they are advanced enough to read).
   - If the students are unable to read, assist with putting the students in order and then have a student volunteer repeat the verse and "tag" another student. (Candy to all participants.)

Students learning the memory verse using this drill.
Photo by Steve Parker

> "When using idioms the students will feel like they are really speaking like a native."

Optional Activity (If Time and English Level Allows): American Idioms

Teenagers everywhere love slang. We discovered this when we had the privilege of hosting a group of teenagers from Belarus here in the United States. When we accompanied their translator to a large bookstore, the book that their translator found most interesting and desirable was a book on American idioms! Your students will also find it interesting if you can teach them some slang or use idioms. An idiom is defined as a "manner of speaking that is natural to a native speaker of a language."(www.audioenglish.net) When using idioms, the students will feel like they are really speaking like a native!

We have incorporated some common idioms as optional activities in these lessons. You will find that your students will enthusiastically embrace lessons that incorporate this principle. I'm sure that your team will be able to think of many other applicable idioms. Use these as starting points and have fun with them!

"In the Dark"

- Sometimes English words and phrases can have more than one meaning. For instance, when you close your eyes and it is dark you are "in the dark." At night when the lights are turned out, you are again "in the dark."
- In English, the phrase, "in the dark," can also mean that a person doesn't understand something. For instance, when you speak to me in your language, I'm "in the dark"; I don't understand!

Conclusion

- Now that we have met each other, we want to go back to the beginning. Since we've looked at what country we are from, now let's look at where we really all came from.

- Where did we *really* come from—way back in the beginning? Let's imagine what it was like!
- Everybody close their eyes—imagine that it is getting darker and darker. Imagine that it is before you were born, before your parents were born, and before their parents were born. Keep your eyes closed and imagine it is before *anybody* was born! There was nothing here except darkness! (Put up the "creation circle, day one, with black felt over the top of it.) If you've imagined how it would be like with nothing here at all, then you can open your eyes!
- Here is what God, in His book, the Bible, says about that time:

  In the beginning God created the heavens and the earth. The earth was without form and void; and darkness was on the face of the deep. And the Spirit of God was hovering over the face of the waters. Then God said, "Let there be light"; and there was light. And God saw the light, that it was good; and God divided the light from the darkness. God called the light Day, and the darkness He called Night. So the evening and the morning were the first day. (Genesis 1:1–5)

- The Bible teaches us that God was always here. He was here before the world began. As He moved in the darkness and emptiness, He decided to create the world!
- How did He do this? It was amazing! God was able to create by just speaking the words! The Bible tells us that He simply said, "Let there be light" and then there was light! (Move black flannel to reveal first day creation circle.) On this first day, God created light in the darkness and organized the light and darkness into day and night.
- As we study these lessons, we will show you what God created each day in the week of creation.
- Practice memory verse again with entire group: "In the beginning God created the heavens and the earth" (Genesis 1:1).
- We have now come to the end of the first day of creation! The very beginning of everything we see in this world today—of you, me, birds, fish, trees, flowers, rivers, and mountains—everything! It was on this first day that God, our Creator, drew near and said, "Let there be light."
- We are all here today because of this first day!
- Close the lesson with a prayer thanking God for this day.

English Lesson Two

Theme: Creation Day Two—God Created the Sky

Review

Each day, spend some time reviewing the lesson from the previous day.

Verse from Day One

- Teacher: "Where did everything come from?"
- Group: "In the beginning God created the heavens and the earth" (Genesis 1:1).
- Practice dialogue one with a selected student (with a prize for participation).
- Practice dialogue two with a selected student (with a prize for participation).
- Practice dialogue three with a selected student (with a prize for participation).
- Practice dialogue four with a selected student (with a prize for participation).
- Teacher: "What did God create on the first day?"
- Group: "Light and day and night."

Materials Needed

- Flannel board with creation circle for day two
- Prizes for review students
- Toy airplane
- Paper to make paper airplanes
- Crayons to color airplanes
- Pictures representing the prepositions
- Poster paper and markers
- Candy, stickers, pencils, pens, and/or small toys
- 8½-by-11-inch card stock to write Bible verse words

Objectives

At the end of lesson two, students will:

- Demonstrate an understanding of the vocabulary words in this lesson.
- Be able to sing the song, "This is the day that the Lord hath made."
- Repeat the memory verse for the day: "The heavens declare the glory of God" (Psalm 19:1).
- Discuss what God did on the second day of creation.
- Have a working knowledge of at least five prepositions.

Introduction

- Today we will learn about day two of creation and have some fun learning English that relates to the creation of day two.
- Does anybody know what God created on the second day?
- The Bible tells us that God created the sky on the second day of creation. This is what it says:

  Then God said, "Let there be a firmament in the midst of the waters, and let it divide the waters from the waters." Thus God made the firmament, and divided the waters which were under the firmament from the waters which were above the firmament; and it was so. And God called the firmament Heaven. So the evening and the morning were the second day (Genesis 1:6–8).

- Once again, God shows His power on day 2. He spoke the words and the sky was created!

Activity One—Song to Celebrate the Day

> ### *Vocabulary for Activity One*
> * This
> * Day
> * That
> * Lord
> * Has
> * Made
> * We
> * Will
> * Rejoice
> * Be
> * Glad
> * In
> * It

1. **Introduce Vocabulary**

    *   Write the words on the board.
    *   Review the words with the students.

2. **Model Song/Comprehension Check**

    Teachers model by singing the song

    *   Teacher A: "This is the day."
    *   Teacher B repeats: "This is the day."
    *   Teacher A: "that the Lord has made."
    *   Teacher B: "that the Lord has made."
    *   Teacher A: "We will rejoice."
    *   Teacher B: "We will rejoice."
    *   Teacher A: "and be glad in it."
    *   Teacher B: "and be glad in it."
    *   Teacher A and B: "This is the day that the Lord has made. We will rejoice and be glad in it."
    *   Teacher A: "This is the day."
    *   Teacher B: "This is the day."
    *   Teacher A and B: "That the Lord has made."

We used a children's chorus for this activity. This chorus is based on Psalm 118:24. It requires a response, which makes it appropriate to use in this setting. If you or your team is not familiar with this chorus, you can search for it online prior to your trip.

There are also examples of choirs singing this song online, as well as the lyrics with guitar chords. These are very useful tools to use when preparing for a mission trip.

- First singer: "This is the day."
- Second singer repeats: "This is the day."
- First singer: "that the Lord has made."
- Second singer repeats: "that the Lord has made."
- First singer: "We will rejoice."
- Second singer: "We will rejoice."
- First singer: "and be glad in it."
- Second singer: "and be glad in it."
- Everyone together: "This is the day that the Lord has made. We will rejoice and be glad in it."
- First singer: "This is the day."
- Second singer "This is the day."
- Everyone together: "That the Lord has made."

3. **Repetition of Song**

- Divide students into two groups.
- Ask for a student volunteer to lead each group along with one of the teachers.
- Have students stand and sing the song back and forth between the two groups.

The students enjoy learning a song in English.
Photo by Steve Parker

Activity Two—Prepositions in Sentences

- We're going to learn some words that help describe where things are. Since God made the sky on day two of creation, we are going to use the sky to help us learn words that describe where things are and then use the same words to describe something else that you see in the room.
- Today we use the sky for airplanes to fly. That's how we got here— on a very long airplane ride! Does anyone want to guess how long it takes to fly from America to your home here?
- What is a preposition?
- Prepositions show relationships between certain words in a sentence. (You may not necessarily use the term *preposition*.)

Vocabulary for Activity Two

- Sky
- Cloud
- Airplane
- Water
- Book
- Flew
- Over
- Under
- Behind
- Through
- Into
- Between
- From the list of common prepositions below, choose five or six that you would like to illustrate to the class. Since we wanted to illustrate prepositions by using things that an airplane can do to a cloud, we choose the following five:
  - ▷ Over
  - ▷ Under
  - ▷ Through
  - ▷ Between
  - ▷ Behind

(The most common prepositions: about, above, across, after, against, along, among, around, at, before, behind, below, beneath, beside, between, beyond, but, by, despite, down, during, except, for, from, in, inside, into, like, near, of, off, on, onto, out, outside, over, past, since, through, throughout, till, to, toward, under, underneath, until, up, upon, with, within, and without.)

1. **Introduce Vocabulary**
   - Write the words on the board.
   - Review the words with the students.

2. **Model/Comprehension Check**
   - Teacher A/Teacher B demonstrate prepositions using sentences that show the airplane/cloud relationship.
     - "The airplane flew *over* the cloud."
     - "The airplane flew *under* the cloud."
     - "The airplane flew *through* the cloud."
     - "The airplane flew *between* the clouds."
     - "The airplane flew *behind* the cloud."

3. **Repetition**
   - Assist students in making paper airplanes.
   - Repeat with students demonstrating the relationship with paper airplanes.

4. **Drill**
   - Show pictures demonstrating the various prepositions, and have students stand and identify the correct word to go with the pictures.
   - Practice with objects in the room (books, pencils, and so on), and add these objects to vocabulary list.

Activity Three—Connect Today's Lesson to the Second Creation Day

Dialogue for Activity Three

"The heavens declare the glory of God" (Psalm 19:1).

Vocabulary for Activity Three

- Heavens
- Declare
- Glory
- God

---

1. **Introduce Vocabulary**

   - Write the words on the board.
   - Review the words with the students.

2. **Model/Comprehension Check**

   - Teacher A: "The heavens declare the glory of God." Psalm 19:1
   - Teacher B: "The heavens declare the glory of God." Psalm 19:1

Teachers model the Bible verse
Picture by Cheryl Parker

3. Repetition of Dialogue between Teacher and Group

- Teacher: "The heavens declare the glory of God" (Psalm 19:1).
- Group: "The heavens declare the glory of God" (Psalm 19:1).

4. Drill

- Select seven students to come to the front of room. Give each student a poster of one of the seven words.
- Mix them up and have students put themselves in order (if they are advanced enough to read).
- If the students are unable to read, assist with putting the students in order and then have a student volunteer repeat the verse and "tag" another student. (Candy to all participants.)

Optional Activity (If Time and English Level Allows): American Idioms

Today we will look at some American idioms that contain prepositions that we studied!

"Water under the Bridge"

- When we say "water under the bridge," it can mean literally that water is under the bridge. However, as a slang expression, it means anything from the past that isn't significant or important anymore. If someone has done something to hurt you, and you have forgiven that person, you can say that whatever that person did is now "water under the bridge."

"Over My Dead Body"

- When someone says "over my dead body," they actually mean that they absolutely will not allow something to happen.

"On the Fence"

- The literal meaning of "on the fence" would mean that something or someone is actually sitting on a fence! However, the expression "on the fence" as an idiom means that a person is undecided about something.

Conclusion

- Let's look again at what happened on the second day of creation.
- God created our sky! On this day God was getting the world ready for the next things that He was going to create. He had to create a place for all the animals, plants, and people that would be here soon. He created the air so that they could live. He knew ahead of time just exactly what would be needed and made it perfectly.
- The Bible tells us that the second day was now ending. So far, in the first two days of creation, we have seen God create light and the sky. There was still no land, no living creature, nothing but water and air! But God knew that all was ready for the next step of creation. I'm sure you are wondering what comes next! What do you think it will be? In our next lesson, we will look and see what God did on the third day!
- Close the lesson with a prayer thanking God for this day.

English Lesson Three

Theme: Creation Day Three—God Created the Earth, Seas, Grass, Plants, and Fruit

Review
Verse from Day One
- Teacher: "Where did everything come from?"
- Group: "In the beginning God created the heavens and the earth" (Genesis 1:1).

Verse from Day Two
- Teacher: "What did God make on the second day of creation?"
- Group: "Sky!"
- Teacher: "What verse helps us remember the second day of creation?"
- Group: "The heavens declare the glory of God" (Psalm 19:1).

Prepositions
- Student demonstration of prepositions: over, under, around, through, between (prize for participation).

Song
- Group: "This is the Day."

Materials Needed
Prior to this lesson, ask your translator what types of fruits and vegetables are available in the area where you are ministering. Fruits and vegetables that you are familiar with may not even be available in the country where you are teaching this lesson. Adjust your lesson to use common fruits and vegetables with which your students will be familiar.

The "bingo" cards and activity need some explanation also. Prior to the trip, our team made a game similar to bingo. However, in place of the letters across the top of the card, we put colors. In place of the numbers on a regular bingo card, we put various fruits and vegetables. There are Internet programs available that will help you make your own personalized bingo cards. (See appendix B.)

When you play the game, pass out the cards to each student. If there are not enough cards, put the students in groups of two or three, with one card for each group. Also, pass out something that the students can use to cover the bingo squares. This can be cardboard square cutouts, dried beans, or even pennies. When planning this game, decide on what will work best for you and your team. The teacher will have access to two containers—one that has colors written on pieces of paper and another that will have the various fruits and vegetables. The teacher will then call out a color and a vegetable such as "red" and "banana." The student will then look across and find the red column. If a banana is in the red column, then the student will cover that square. The game continues until someone gets a horizontal or vertical line filled—just like bingo! Variations of this game can be "cover the four corners" or "cover the entire card". Be prepared with prizes for the winning students!

- Fruit or pictures of fruit
- Vegetables or pictures of vegetables
- Grocery sacks
- "Bingo" cards and markers
- Candy, pencils, pens, small toys, and/or stickers
- Flannel board and day three circle

Objectives

At the end of lesson three, students will:

- Demonstrate an understanding of the vocabulary words in this lesson.
- Repeat the memory verse for the day: "My help comes from the Lord, the maker of heaven and earth" (Psalm 121:2 GWT).
- Discuss what God did on the third day of creation.
- Identify fruit and vegetables.
- Identify Colors.

Introduction

- Today we are going to look at what God did on the third day of creation.
- Does anybody know?
- So far, we have a world with water and sky—that's all!
- The Bible tells us that on the third day, God looked down, and this is what He did:

Then God said, "Let the waters under the heavens be gathered together into one place, and let the dry land appear"; and it was so. And God called the dry land Earth, and the gathering together of the waters He called Seas. And God saw that it was good. Then God said, "Let the earth bring forth grass, the herb that yields seed, and the fruit tree that yields fruit, whose seed is in itself according to its kind. And God saw that it was good. So the evening and the morning were the third day" (Genesis 1:9–13)

Activity One: Food—Fruit

Vocabulary for Activity One

- Fruit:
  - ▷ Apple
  - ▷ Banana
  - ▷ Grapes
  - ▷ Lemon
  - ▷ Orange
  - ▷ Pear
  - ▷ Peach
  - ▷ Pineapple
- I
- Want
- Eat
- Something
- What
- Do
- You
- Like
- Would
- Let's
- An (a)

Dialogue for Activity One

A. "I want to eat something."
B. "What do you want?"
A. "I would like to eat an apple (or other fruit)."
B. "Okay. Let's eat an apple."

1. **Introduce Vocabulary**
   - Write the words on the board.
   - Review the words with the students.

2. **Model/Comprehension Check**
   - Teacher A: "I want to eat something."
   - Teacher B: "What do you want?"

- Teacher A: "I would like to eat an apple (or other fruit)."
- Teacher B: "Okay. Let's eat an apple."

3. Repetition of Dialogue between Teacher and Group

- Teacher: "I want to eat something."
- Group: "I want to eat something."
- Teacher: "What do you want?"
- Group: "What do you want?"
- Teacher: "I would like to eat an apple."
- Group: "I would like to eat an apple."
- Teacher: "Okay, let's eat an apple."
- Group: "Okay, let's eat an apple."

Repetition with Response

- Teacher: "I want to eat something."
- Group: "What do you want?"
- Teacher: "I would like to eat an apple."
- Group: "Okay. Let's eat an apple."

Repeat the dialogue using other fruits.

4. Drill

- Divide students into three circles with fruit or pictures of fruit in the middle.
- Chain drill:
  - ▷ First student: "I want to eat something."
  - ▷ Second student: "What do you want?"
  - ▷ First student: "I would like to eat a(an) _____." (The first student goes to middle of the circle and picks the correct fruit.)
  - ▷ Second student: "Okay. Let's eat a(an) _____ (same fruit)."
  - ▷ Second student to third student: "I want to eat something." (The second student puts back the previous fruit.)
  - ▷ Third student: "What do you want?" Etc.

Activity Two: Food—Vegetable

Vocabulary for Activity Two

- Vegetables: (Add vegetables to the
  vocabulary list, but also continue
  with fruit for this exercise.)
  ▷ Carrot
  ▷ Tomato
  ▷ Corn
  ▷ Broccoli
  ▷ Potato

Dialogue for Activity Two

A. "We need to go to the market."
B. "What do we need to buy?"
A. "We need vegetables and fruit."
B. "Okay. Let's buy some potatoes and apples (or _____ and
_____)."

1. **Introduce Vocabulary**
   - Write the words on the board.
   - Review the words with the students.

2. **Model/Comprehension Check**
   - Teacher A: "We need to go to the market."
   - Teacher B: "What do we need to buy?"
   - Teacher A: "We need vegetables and fruit."
   - Teacher B: "Okay. Let's buy some potatoes and apples (or
     _____ and _____)."

3. **Repetition of Dialogue between Teacher and Group**
   - Teacher: "We need to go to the market."
   - Group: "We need to go to the market."
   - Teacher: "What do we need to buy?"
   - Group: "What do we need to buy?"
   - Teacher: "We need vegetables and fruit."
   - Group: "We need vegetables and fruit."
   - Teacher: "Okay. Let's buy some potatoes and apples."

Repetition with Response

- Teacher: "We need to go to the market."
- Group: "What do we need to buy?"
- Teacher: "We need vegetables and fruit."
- Group: "Okay. Let's buy some potatoes and apples (or _____ and _____)."

4. **Drill**

- Divide the class into three circles.
- Place "market" items in the middle of the circle.
- The teacher takes a shopping bag and starts the drill.
- Teacher: Let's go to the market and buy some fruits and vegetables. What do you want to buy?
- The first student will identify a fruit or vegetable to place in the bag and say. First student: Let's buy a (an) _____."
  The student will then place that item in the bag and pass the shopping bag to the next student.
- The teacher can then ask the next student: What do you want to buy?
- The 2nd student will take the bag and say "Let's buy a(an) (name the first item and add to it) and a (an) _____.
- Continue with this passing the bag and asking each student until the bag is full.

Activity Three: Colors

Vocabulary for Activity Three
- Red
- Pink
- Orange
- Green
- Blue
- Purple
- Black
- White
- Gray
- Brown
- Favorite
- Color

Dialogue for Activity Three

A. "Do you have a favorite color?"
B. "My favorite color is _____."

1. **Introduce Vocabulary**
   - Write the words on the board.
   - Review the words with the students.

2. **Model/Comprehension Check**
   - Teacher A: "Do you have a favorite color?"
   - Teacher B: "My favorite color is _____."

3. **Repetition of Dialogue between Teacher and Group**
   - Teacher: "Do you have a favorite color?"
   - Group: "Do you have a favorite color?"
   - Teacher: "My favorite color is _____ (choose a color)."
   - Group: "My favorite color is _____ (repeats color)."

Repetition with Response

- Ask each student the following individually around the room.
- Teacher: "Do you have a favorite color?"
- Student: "My favorite color is _____."

4. Drill

Fruit/Vegetable Color Bingo

- Pass out "bingo" cards to students and markers to cover the cards.
- Call out a color and then a fruit/vegetable (refer to bingo instructions in the introduction of this lesson).
- Can be played multiple times. If desired, you can change the game to cover a horizontal, vertical, or diagonal line each time.
- Provide candy and/or prizes to the winner of each game.

Activity Four—Connect Today's Lesson to the Third Day of Creation

- We've been studying all the things that God created on the third day of creation. Now let's learn a verse to help us remember this day.

> *Vocabulary for Activity Four*
> - Help
> - Comes
> - Lord
> - Who

Dialogue for Activity Four

A. "My help comes from the Lord, who made heaven and earth" (Psalm 121:2).

1. **Introduce Vocabulary**
   - Write the words on the board.
   - Review the words with the students.

2. **Model/Comprehension Check**
   - Teacher A: "My help comes from the Lord, who made heaven and earth." (Psalm 121:2)
   - Teacher B: My help comes from the Lord, who made the heaven and earth." (Psalm 121:2)
   -

3. **Repetition of Dialogue between Teacher and Group**
   - Teacher: "My help comes from the Lord, who made heaven and earth" (Psalm 121:2).
   - Group: "My help comes from the Lord, who made heaven and earth" (Psalm 121:2).

4. **Drill**
   - Ask individual students to volunteer to recite the verse. (Give candy to those who can say the verse.)

Optional Activity (If Time and English Level Allows): American Idioms

Since we talked about food today, let's look at a couple of idioms that are based on food.

"A Piece of Cake"

- A piece of cake can be just that, a literal piece of cake! But when a person says that something that's not cake is "a piece of cake," that person is referring to a task that can be accomplished very easily. If you are finding these lessons very easy, then you can say that our English lessons are a "piece of cake!"

"Apple of My Eye"

- If a person refers to someone as the "apple of my eye," that means the person is loved very much and cherished above all others.

Conclusion

- Let's all listen to what the Bible has to say about this third day of creation. It was very early and very quiet on the third day. So far, all we had was water and sky. Then God spoke again:

   And God said, "Let the waters under the heavens be gathered together into one place, and let the dry land appear." (Genesis 1:9)

- What happened when He said that?
- Suddenly, the water started moving. It was the first storm! The waves must have been very big, and the first wind ever began to blow. Have any of you ever been in the middle of a storm like this? The wind continued to blow so hard that it blew the water aside, and dry land began to appear! On the third day, God created dry land with hills, mountains, and even sandy beaches all around.
- God wasn't finished with His creation on this day yet. He wanted the world to reflect His majesty and beauty. He did this by speaking again and creating beautiful trees and plants.

   "Let the earth bring forth grass, the herb that yields seed, and the fruit tree that yields fruit according to its kind, whose seed is in itself, on the earth." Genesis 1:11

- Don't forget that He is still thinking about what He will make on the other days. He was preparing food for the animals and for us when He created the fruit trees and plants.
- Wow! God's world reflects His power, His majesty, and His glory. *Put up the third day creation circle.*
- There are breathtaking scenes everywhere now! Have you ever walked outside and enjoyed the beauty of nature? Have you ever taken a hike to a mountain or a lake that is surrounded by beautiful plants? Have you ever looked up into the sky at night or seen the beautiful sunrise in the morning or the sunset in the evening? When you do these things, you can get a small glimpse of how big and powerful

33

- The Bible describes the end of the day like this: "So the evening and the morning were the third day" (Genesis 1:13).
- It will be another exciting day tomorrow!
- *Close the lesson in prayer thanking God for this day.*

English Lesson Four

Theme: Creation, Day Four—God Created the Sun, Moon, and Stars

Materials Needed

Prior to the trip, our team made a word search puzzle. This consisted of drawing a box with individual squares for each letter. Then we placed the vocabulary words in the box, one letter in each square. We then put random letters in each of the blank squares so that the student would need to search for the words. As students identify words, they will circle them. All the vocabulary words that are in the puzzle are listed at the bottom of the page so that the student will know what words to look for in the puzzle. There are free Internet programs that can assist you in making a word search game. (See appendix B.)

A variety of calendars can be collected prior to the trip to use in this lesson. Many calendars have beautiful pictures of places in America that will be of interest to your students. The calendars are also good gifts for your group to leave for the students.

The calendar quiz sheets should also be made ahead of time. There are also free Internet programs that can assist you in making a calendar quiz. (See appendix B.)

- Calendars
- Calendar quiz sheet
- Candy, pencils, pens, small toys, and/or stickers
- Word puzzle game
- Pencils or pens for game
- Cards for the verse (8-½-by-11-inch card stock paper and black markers)
- Flannel board and day four creation circle

Review

Verse from Day One

- Teacher: "Where did everything come from?"
- Group: "In the beginning God created the heavens and the earth" (Genesis 1:1).

Verse from Day Two

- Teacher: "What did God make on day two?"
- Group: "Sky!"
- Teacher: "What verse reminds us that God created the sky?"
- Group: "The heavens declare the glory of God" (Psalm 19:1).

Verse from Day Three

- Teacher: "What verse did we learn to help us remember the third day of creation?"
- Group: "My help comes from the Lord, who made heaven and earth" (Psalm 121:2).

Colors, Fruits, and Vegetables:

- Go around room with the following dialogue:
- First student: "I am going to the market and buy a(n) (red) (apple)" (or any color and any fruit/vegetable).
- First student to second student: "What are you going to buy?"
- Second student: "I am going to the market to buy a(n) (green) (broccoli)."
- Second student to third student: "What are you going to buy?" Etc.

Song

- Group: "This is the Day."

Objectives

At the end of lesson four, students will:

- Demonstrate an understanding of the vocabulary words in this lesson.
- Repeat the memory verse for the day: "The day is Yours, the night also is Yours; You have prepared the light and the sun" (Psalm 74:16).

- Discuss what God did on the fourth day of creation.
- Recite the days of the week and the months of the year.
- Recite ordinal and cardinal numbers one through thirty-one.

Introduction

- Today we are going to look at what God made on the fourth day of creation. Does anybody know?
- In just three days, we have gone from a dark space to a land full of beauty. We have plants, grass, and all kinds of fruits and vegetables, just as you all were discussing a few minutes ago. Let's look at what happened next!

Then God said, "Let there be lights in the firmament of the heavens to divide the day from the night; and let them be for signs and seasons, and for days and years; and let them be for lights in the firmament of the heavens to give light on the earth"; and it was so. Then God made two great lights; the greater light to rule the day, and the lesser light to rule the nights. He made the stars also. God set them in the firmament of the heavens to give light on the earth, and to rule over the day and over the night, and to divide the light from the darkness. And God saw that it was good. So the evening and the morning were the fourth day. (Genesis 1:14–19)

- God knew that without the sun and moon, the plants could not last very long. Plants need light and warmth just like the animals and people that God would soon make.
- From the beginning of time until now, He planned not only the day and night, but also the seasons and the years!
- Let's look at the days, nights, and seasons and practice English words and sentences that help us understand the calendar that God set up way back in the beginning of time!

Activity One

Vocabulary for Activity One

Days of the Week

- Sunday
- Monday
- Tuesday
- Wednesday
- Thursday
- Friday
- Saturday

Other Terms Referring to Days

- Today
- Tomorrow
- Yesterday

Dialogue for Activity One

A. "What day is today?"
B. "Today is _____."
A. "What day is tomorrow?"
B. "Tomorrow is _____."
A. "What day was yesterday?"
B. "Yesterday was _____."

Repeat, starting with a different day (pointing to the calendar during the dialogue).

1. **Introduce Vocabulary**
   - Write the words on the board.
   - Review the words with the students.

2. **Model/Comprehension Check**
   - Teacher A: "What day is today?"
   - Teacher B: "Today is _____."
   - Teacher A: "What day is tomorrow?"
   - Teacher B: "Tomorrow is _____."

- Teacher A: "What day was yesterday?"
- Teacher B: "Yesterday was _____."

3. Repetition of Dialogue between Teacher and Group

- Teacher: "What day is today?"
- Group: "What day is today?"
- Teacher: "Today is _____."
- Group: "Today is _____."
- Teacher: "What day is tomorrow?"
- Group: "What day is tomorrow?"
- Teacher: "Tomorrow is _____."
- Group: "Tomorrow is _____."
- Teacher: "What was yesterday?"
- Group: "What was yesterday?"
- Teacher: "Yesterday was _____."
- Group: "Yesterday was _____."

Repetition with Response

- Teacher: "What day is today?"
- Group: "Today is _____?"
- Teacher: "What day is tomorrow?"
- Group: "Tomorrow is _____?"
- Teacher: "What day was yesterday?"
- Group: "Yesterday was _____?"

4. Drill

Calendar Quiz

- Divide class into three or four teams. Ask questions from the calendar quiz sheet.
- The first student to stand and get the correct answer gets ten points.
- The team with the most points wins. (All winning team members get a piece of candy.)

Activity Two

> ### *Vocabulary for Activity Two*
> *Months of the Year*
> - January
> - February
> - March
> - April
> - May
> - June
> - July
> - August
> - September
> - October
> - November
> - December
>
> *Additional Word*
> - Birthday

Dialogue for Activity Two

A. "When is your birthday?"
B. "My birthday is in _____. When is your birthday?"
A. "My birthday is in _____."

1. **Introduce Vocabulary**
   - Write the vocabulary on the board.
   - Review the words with the students.

2. **Model/Comprehension Check**
   - Teacher A: "When is your birthday?"
   - Teacher B: "My birthday is in _____. When is your birthday?"
   - Teacher A: "My birthday is in _____."

3. **Repetition of Dialogue between Teacher and Group**
   - Teacher: "When is your birthday?"

- Group: "When is your birthday?"
- Teacher: "My birthday is in _____. When is your birthday?"
- Group: "My birthday is in _____. When is your birthday?"
- Teacher: "My birthday is in _____."
- Group: "My birthday is in _____."

Repetition with Response

- Teacher: "When is your birthday?"
- Group: "My birthday is in _____. When is your birthday?"
- Teacher: "My birthday is in _____."

4. Drill

- Divide students into their birthday months (up to twelve groups).
- Pass out the word puzzle game.
- The birthday group to have someone first complete the puzzle (or that has the person who gets the most in a certain time period) wins the game!

Activity Three

Vocabulary for Activity Three
- Numbers one to thirty-one
- Ordinal
  ▷ Ordinal numbers tell the order of things: first, second, third, etc.
- Cardinal
  ▷ Cardinal numbers tell the quantity, or "how many": one, two, three, four, etc.

Dialogue for Activity Three

A. "My birthday is _____ the _____ (April the ninth, for example). What day is your birthday?"
B. "My Birthday is _____ the _____."

1. Introduce Vocabulary

- Write the cardinal numbers on the board.
- Write the ordinal numbers on the board.
- Review the words with the students.

2. Model/Comprehension Check

- Teacher A: "My birthday is _____ the _____ (April the ninth, for example). What day is your birthday?"
- Teacher B. "My Birthday is _____ the _____."

3. Repetition of Dialogue between Teacher and Group

(For this exercise, it may be more effective to do this with individual students instead of the group as a whole.)

- Teacher: "My birthday is _____ the _____. What day is your birthday?"
- Student: "My birthday is _____ the _____. What day is your birthday?"
- Teacher: "My birthday is _____ the _____."
- Student: "My birthday is _____ the _____."

Repetition of Dialogue with Response

- Teacher: "My birthday is _____ the _____. What day is your birthday?"
- Student: "My birthday is _____ the _____."

4. Drill

- Put the big calendar at the front of the room.
- Call all students with January birthdays up. Have them each find their day and put their name on the calendar stating "My birthday is _____ the _____."
- Repeat for each month that is represented in the class.

Activity Four—Connect Today's Lesson to the Third Day of Creation

On the fourth day of creation, the sun, moon, and stars were completed and placed in the sky! The verse that we are going to learn today tells us that God made the day and the night. It goes like this:

Dialogue for Activity Four

"The day is Yours, the night also is Yours; You have prepared the light and the sun" (Psalm 74:16).

1. **Introduce the Verse and the New Vocabulary**
    *   Write it on the board
    *   Review the words with the students.

2. **Model/Comprehension Check**
    *   Teacher A: "The day is Yours, the night also is Yours; You have prepared the light and the sun" (Psalm 74:16).
    *   Teacher B: "The day is Yours, the night also is Yours; You have prepared the light and the sun" (Psalm 74:16).

3. **Repetition**
    *   Teacher: "The day is Yours, the night also is Yours; You have prepared the light and the sun" (Psalm 74:16).
    *   *Group:* "The day is Yours, the night also is Yours; You have prepared the light and the sun" (Psalm 74:16).

4. **Drill**
    *   Pass out the large cards, with one word from today's verse per card, to seventeen students.
    *   Have the students line up in the right order.
    *   Have the students lead the group in repeating the verse.

Optional Activity

Have the class divide into two teams. Create a contest atmosphere and offer prizes to the team that sings the loudest. (You may end up giving candy to everyone!) When it is each team's turn to sing, the students on that team stand up. When the other team is singing, the first team's students sit down. If you are not familiar with this chorus, you can find it in the public domain of the Internet and familiarize your team with it prior to the trip. This is a good song to sing at any time that the class needs a break from sitting!

Song: "Alleluia, Praise Ye the Lord"

Team 1: "Allelu, allelu, allelu, alleluia"
Team 2: "Praise ye the Lord!"
Team 1: "Allelu, allelu, allelu, alleluia"
Team 2: "Praise ye the Lord!"
Team 2: "Praise ye the Lord!"
Team 1: "Alleluia!"
Team 2: "Praise ye the Lord!"
Team 1: "Alleluia!"
Team 2: "Praise ye the Lord!"
Team 1: "Alleluia!"
Everybody: "Praise ye the Lord!"

Optional Activity (If Time and English Level Allows): American Idioms

The idioms that we will look at today have to do with nighttime since the verse we learned today teaches us that the night time belongs to God!

"Blue Moon"

- The term "blue moon" means that something is a rare event or a rare occurrence. We could say that something happens only once in a "blue moon." If we took these words literally, we would be saying that the moon was the color blue!

"Hit the Sack"

- A slang term for going to bed at night is "hit the sack." When someone is very tired, he may say, "I'm going to hit the sack." That means that he is going to go to bed! If we took these words literally, they would mean that he would actually take a sack and hit it with his fist!

Conclusion

- God set up the system of time that we know today. We have day and night, light and darkness, all divided into 24-hour days, 7-day weeks, 365-day years, and 4 seasons.
- God was in the process of making the world so that the human beings He created would not only have a beautiful place to live, but also would have an orderly place to live.
- This system of time that God created allows us to have times of rest and worship. God planned it this way.
- "So the evening and the morning were the fourth day" (Genesis 1:19).
- *Close this lesson with prayer thanking God for this day.*

English Lesson Five

Theme: Creation Day Five—God Created the Birds and the Fish

Review

Verse from Day One
- Teacher: "Where did everything come from?"
- Group: "In the beginning God created the heavens and the earth" (Genesis 1:1).

Verse from Day Two
- Teacher: "What did God make on day two?"
- Group: "Sky!"
- Teacher: "What verse reminds us that God created the sky?"
- Group: "The heavens declare the glory of God" (Psalm 19:1).

Verse from Day Three
- Teacher: "What verse did we learn to help us remember the third day of creation?"
- Group: "My help comes from the Lord, who made heaven and earth" (Psalm 121:2).

Verse from Day Four
- Teacher: "What verse helps us remember that God made the day and the night?"
- Group: "The day is Yours, the night also is Yours; You have prepared the light and the sun" (Psalm 74:16).

Lesson Four Review
- Review the days of week: the group recites together.

- Review the months of year: the group recites together.
- Review the ordinal numbers: the group recites together to thirty-first.
- Review the cardinal numbers: the group recites together to thirty-one.

Materials Needed

Prior to the trip, our team made packs of "concentration" cards from the vocabulary words or pictures of vocabulary words (such as fruits and vegetables) that we would be using in this lesson. This can be easily done on a computer, printed on heavy paper, backed with colored construction paper, and laminated at an office supply store. Once laminated, cut the cards apart to make a "deck" of cards with a vocabulary word on each card. (See appendix B.)

Small cardboard boxes can also be purchased or collected from team members. These boxes should be about the size of a coffee mug box or a little larger. They can be prepared ahead of time with pictures on the sides for the "spin the bottle" game. They can be flat for traveling and put together with tape after your team has arrived.

- Flannel board with creation circle for day five
- Pictures of fish and chicken
- Concentration cards (three packs)
- 8-½-by-11-inch card stock and black markers for verse word cards
- Boxes with pictures for "spin the bottle"
- Candy, pencils, pens, small toys, and/or stickers
- Empty soft drink bottle for "spin the bottle"

Objectives

At the end of lesson five, students will:

- Demonstrate an understanding of the vocabulary words in this lesson.
- Repeat the memory verse for the day: "Follow Me, and I will make you fishers of men" (Matthew 4:19).
- Discuss what God did on the fifth day of creation.
- Be able to identify the difference between "like" and "don't like."
- Sing the song, "Deep and Wide."

Introduction

- God had made a beautiful world! However, the only sounds so far were the wind rustling through the leaves and the waves beating on the seashore! God looked around and knew that He was not finished! This is what the Bible says happened on the fifth day:

Then God said, "Let the waters abound with an abundance of living creatures, and let birds fly above the earth across the face of the firmament of the heavens." So God created great sea creatures and every living thing that moves, with which the waters abounded, according to their kind, and every winged bird according to its kind. And God saw that it was good. And God blessed them, saying, "Be fruitful and multiply, and fill the waters in the seas, and let birds multiply on the earth." So the evening and the morning were the fifth day. (Genesis 1:20–23)

Activity One: Identify "Like" and "Don't Like"

> ### Vocabulary for Activity One
> - Fish
> - Chicken
> - Eggs
> - Like
> - Don't
> - Eat
> - Where

Dialogue for Activity One

A. "Do you like fish?"
B. "Yes, I do," or "No, I don't."
A. "Do you like chicken?"
B. "Yes, I do," or "No, I don't."
A. Where can I buy some chicken and fish?
B. You can buy chicken and fish at the market.

1. **Introduce Vocabulary**
   - Write the words on the board.
   - Show students the pictures of fish and chicken.
   - Review the words with the students.

2. **Model/Comprehension Check**
   - Teacher A: "Do you like fish?"
   - Teacher B: "Yes, I do," or "No, I don't."
   - Teacher A: "Do you like chicken?"
   - Teacher B: "Yes, I do," or "No, I don't."
   - Teacher A: Where can I buy some chicken and fish?
   - Teacher B: You can buy chicken and fish at the market.

3. **Repetition of Dialogue between Teacher and Group**
   - Teacher: "Do you like fish?"
   - Group: "Do you life fish?"
   - Teacher: "Yes, I do," or "No, I don't."
   - Group: "Yes, I do," or "No, I don't."
   - Teacher: "Do you like chicken?"
   - Group: "Do you like chicken?"
   - Teacher: "Yes, I do," or "No, I don't."
   - Group: "Yes, I do," or "No, I don't."
   - Teacher: "Where can I buy some chicken and fish?"
   - Group: "Where can I buy some chicken and fish?"
   - Teacher: "You can buy chicken and fish at the market."
   - Group: "You can buy chicken and fish at the market."

   Repetition of Dialogue with Response
   - Teacher: "Do you like fish?"
   - Group: "Yes, I do," or "No, I don't."
   - Teacher: "Do you like chicken?"
   - Group: "Yes, I do," or "No, I don't."
   - Teacher: "Where can I buy some chicken and fish?"
   - Group: "You can buy chicken and fish at the market."

4. **Drill: "Spin the Bottle"**
   - Divide the group into three or four circles.

- Take out the bottle and the box with pictures of words on its sides.
- Roll the box and spin the bottle. Have the student that the bottle points to make a sentence with the word that comes up on top.
- Repeat until all students have made sentences.

Activity Two: Song: "Deep and Wide"

Once again, we chose a children's chorus to use in this lesson. Because there are so few words in this song, it is ideal to teach very quickly! Since there are hand motions, it gets the class involved, up, and active! If you do not know this children's, chorus you can find it on the Internet and learn it prior to your trip.

> ### *Vocabulary for Activity Two*
> - Deep
> - Depth
> - Wide
> - Fountain
> - Flowing

1. **Introduce Vocabulary**
   - Write the words on the board.
   - Review the words with the students.

2. **Model/Comprehension Check**
   - Teacher A/Teacher B
   - Demonstrate the song, complete with the "hmmmms!"

3. **Repetition**
   - Teacher: "Deep and wide, deep and wide."
   - Group: "Deep and wide, deep and wide."
   - Teacher: "There's a fountain flowing deep and wide."
   - Group: "There's a fountain flowing deep and wide."

51

4. Drill

- Have students stand up and stretch before singing the song.
- Ask for volunteer students to lead along with the teacher.
- Sing with the group following the student leaders and teachers.

Song: "Deep and Wide"

Deep and wide
Deep and wide
There's a fountain flowing deep and wide
Deep and wide
Deep and wide
There's a fountain flowing deep and wide

Hmmm and wide
Hmmm and wide
There's a fountain flowing hmmm and wide
Hmmm and wide
Hmmm and wide
There's a fountain flowing hmmm and wide

Hmmm and hmmm
Hmmm and hmmm
There's a fountain flowing hmmm and hmmm
Hmmm and hmmm
Hmmm and hmmm
There's a fountain flowing hmmm and hmmm

Hmmm and hmmm
Hmmm and hmmm
Hmmm hmmm hmmm hmmm flowing hmmm and hmmm
Hmmm and hmmm
Hmmm and hmmm
Hmmm hmmm hmmm hmmm flowing hmmm and hmmm

Hmmm hmmm hmmm
Hmmm hmmm hmmm
Hmmm hmmm hmmm hmmm hmmm hmmm hmmm hmmm
Hmmm hmmm hmmm
Hmmm hmmm hmmm
Hmmm hmmm hmmm hmmm hmmm hmmm hmmm hmmm

Optional: Another Meaning of the Word "Deep"

So far this week, we have learned some pretty amazing things about how the world began! You've learned about how powerful God is. He just spoke and created the things that we see. The Bible tells us other things about God too. We've just learned the word "deep." The Bible tells us that the oceans are not the only thing that is really deep. The Bible uses the word "deep" to describe God's wisdom and knowledge. It says that His wisdom and knowledge are so deep that no one can understand them!

> Oh, the depth of the riches both of the wisdom and knowledge of God! How unsearchable are His judgments and His ways past finding out! (Romans 11:33).

Activity Three: What Do We Need at the Store?

> ### *Vocabulary for Activity Three*
> - We
> - Need
> - At
> - Store
> - Pounds
> - Of
> - Some
> - Yes
> - Get
> - Dozen

Dialogue for Activity Three

A. "What do we need at the store?"
B. "We need two pounds of fish and some chicken."
A. "Do we need eggs?"
B. "Yes. Please get a dozen."

1. **Introduce Vocabulary**
   - Write the words on the board.
   - Review the words with the students.

2. **Model/Comprehension Check**
   - Teacher A: "What do we need at the store?"
   - Teacher B: "We need two pounds of fish and some chicken."
   - Teacher A: "Do we need eggs?"
   - Teacher B: "Yes. Please get a dozen."

3. **Repetition of Dialogue between Teacher and Group**
   - Teacher: "What do we need at the store?"
   - Group: "What do we need at the store?"
   - Teacher: "We need two pounds of fish and some chicken."
   - Group: "We need two pounds of fish and some chicken."
   - Teacher: "Do we need eggs?"
   - Group: "Do we need eggs?"
   - Teacher: "Yes. Please get a dozen."
   - Group: "Yes. Please get a dozen."

   Repetition with Response
   - Teacher: "What do we need at the store?"
   - Group: "We need two pounds of fish and some chicken."
   - Teacher: "Do we need eggs?"
   - Group: "Yes. Please get a dozen."

4. **Drill**
   - Divide students into three or four groups.
   - Play the memory game with the cards that have the words and/or pictures from the dialogues in this lesson.
   - When a match is made, the student must make a sentence with the matched item.
   - Give the student a prize when she offers a correct sentence.

Students playing the memory game.
Photo by Cheryl Parker

Activity Four—Connect Today's Lesson to the Fifth Day of Creation

- We've been studying the things that God made on the fifth day of creation. Let's learn a verse to help us remember this day.
- God made all the beautiful things that we see on the earth. Tomorrow we will see that He made people also. He made us so that we could love Him and worship Him for all time. His desire for us is to follow Him and love Him with all our hearts. We will learn more about God's plan for human beings in the next two days. Today, the verse that we will learn will help us remember that God wants us to follow Him.
- Today's verse is, "Follow Me, and I will make you fishers of men" (Matthew 4:19).

> ### Vocabulary for Activity Four
> - Follow
> - Me
> - Make
> - Fishers
> - Of
> - Men

1. **Introduce Vocabulary**
   - Write the words on the board.
   - Review the words with the students.

2. **Model/Comprehension Check**
   - Teacher: "Follow Me, and I will make you fishers of men" (Matthew 4:19).

3. **Repetition**
   - Teacher: "Follow Me, and I will make you fishers of men" (Matthew 4:19).
   - Group: "Follow Me, and I will make you fishers of men" (Matthew 4:19).

4. **Drill**
   - Have ten students come up front and give each student a card with a word on it.
   - Ask for a student volunteer to lead the verse.
   - Have the ten students line up themselves in order and then repeat the verse.

Optional Activity (If Time and English Level Allows): American Idioms

Today we will look at some idioms that mention birds, chickens, and eggs!

"A Bird in the Hand is Worth Two in the Bush"

- This idiom is not talking about having a real bird! It's is an expression meaning that having something that is certain is much better than taking a risk for more, because chances are you might lose everything.

"Don't Count Your Chickens Before They Hatch"

- This is not talking about chickens at all! It is an expression that means for you not to depend on something until you are sure of it.

"Don't Put All Your Eggs in One Basket"

- This is an expression that means that you should not put all your resources in one possibility. Spread your resources around into different things and don't count on just one thing making you successful!

Conclusion

- Let's look back over the fifth day of creation. It was an amazing day!
- Can you close your eyes and just imagine being there? What would it have been like to see the first birds flying in the air and the first fish swimming in the ocean? Now there are more sounds! You can hear the birds singing. (Put up the fifth day creation circle.)
- Now open your eyes and see the picture of the fifth day of creation. It's an exciting day, but the best is yet to come!
- The Bible tells that after God finished creating the sea creatures and the birds, the fifth day was over. It says, "So the evening and the morning were the fifth day" (Genesis 1:23).
- *Close the class in prayer thanking God for this day.*

English Lesson Six

Theme: Creation Day Six—God Created Man

Review

Verse from Day One
- Teacher: "Where did everything come from?"
- Group: "In the beginning God created the heavens and the earth" (Genesis 1:1).

Verse from Day Two
- Teacher: "What did God make on day two?"
- Group: "Sky!"
- Teacher: "What verse reminds us that God created the sky?"
- Group: "The heavens declare the glory of God" (Psalm 19:1).

Verse from Day Three
- Teacher: "What verse did we learn to help us remember the third day of creation?"
- Group: "My help comes from the Lord, who made heaven and earth" (Psalm 121:2).

Verse from Day Four
- Teacher: "What verse helps us remember that God made the day and the night?"
- Group: "The day is Yours, the night also is Yours; You have prepared the light and the sun" (Psalm 74:16).

Verse from Day Five

- Teacher: "God made the birds and the fish. He wants us to follow Him and make us fishers of men."
- Group: "Follow Me, and I will make you fishers of men" (Matthew 4:19).

Materials Needed

- Flannel board with creation day six circle
- Candy, pencils, pens, small toys, and/or stickers
- 8-½-by-11-inch card stock and black marker for verse word cards
- Markers and poster board

Prior to the trip, familiarize the team with the two songs that will be used in this lesson, "Head, Shoulders, Knees, and Toes" and the "Hokey Pokey." These songs are readily available online if you are not already familiar with them.

Objectives

At the end of lesson six, students will

- Demonstrate an understanding of the vocabulary words in this lesson.
- Repeat the memory verse for the day: "For I am fearfully and wonderfully made" (Psalm 139:14).
- Discuss what God did on the sixth day of creation.
- Identify major external parts of the body.
- Describe a health problem to the doctor.

Introduction

- Early in the morning on the sixth day, there were many more sounds! God made all the animals and they were loud!
- What are some animals that you like?
- What are some animals that you don't like?
- After He made the animals, God said that it was good, but He was not finished! He wanted someone that He could talk to and be friends with. He wanted to create a companion. So He created us! This is what the Bible said happened:

Then God said, "Let Us make man in Our image, according to Our likeness; let them have dominion over the fish of the sea, over the birds of the air, and over the cattle, over all the earth and over every creeping thing that creeps on the earth." So God created man in His own image; in the image of God He created him; male and female He created them" (Genesis 1:26–27).

- "In His own image!" Human beings were the only creations that God made in His own image. He made us that way so that we could communicate with Him and be friends with Him for all eternity. The next verses tell more about exactly how God made human beings.

"And the Lord God formed man of the dust of the ground" (Genesis 2:7).

- God spoke the rest of the world and all the animals into existence, but God created human beings differently. He actually reached down and formed the first man, Adam, from the dust of the ground. Then the Bible tells us that He leaned down and breathed life into Adam. The Bible says that God "breathed into his nostrils the breath of life; and man became a living soul" (Genesis 2:7b).
- God also made a woman so that Adam wouldn't be alone. God knew that companionship was important to Him and so it would also be important to the man that He had just created. God performed the first surgery! He made Adam fall into a deep sleep and made the woman from one of Adam's ribs. How amazing that God took care of every detail when making both the man and the woman.
- Today we're going to learn the English words for the parts of the body. We'll also learn how to express when something is wrong and how to follow directions from the doctor. So let's get started …

Activity One: Identify Major External Body Parts

Vocabulary for Activity One
- Head
- Shoulder(s)
- Knee(s)
- Arm(s)
- Hand(s)
- Elbow(s)
- Finger(s)
- Wrist
- Stomach
- Ankle(s)
- Foot (Feet)
- Toe(s)
- Eye(s)
- Ear(s)
- Mouth
- Nose
- Hair

No Dialogue

1. **Introduce Vocabulary**
   - Write the words on the board.
   - Review the words with the students.

2. **Model/Comprehension Check**
   - Practice by identifying body parts between the teachers and the group.

3. **Repetition**
   - Ask students to point to their _____.

4. Drill

Songs to Practice Identifying Body Parts

- Teach the students the song, "Head, Shoulders, Knees, and Toes" by demonstrating the song and the actions that go with the song. Ask the students to all stand up, and ensure there is adequate room between students.
- Song: "Head, Shoulders, Knees, and Toes"
  Head, shoulders, knees, and toes,
  knees and toes.
  Head, shoulders, knees, and toes,
  knees and toe-o-o-os.
  Eyes and ears and mouth and nose …
  Head, shoulders, knees, and toes,
  Knees and toes!
- Teach the students the song, "Hokey Pokey," with the class forming a circle around the room.
- Song: "Hokey Pokey"
  You put your right foot in,
  you put your right foot out,
  you put your right foot in,
  and you shake it all about.
  You do the hokey pokey and you turn yourself around.
  That's what it's all about!

Continue singing the "Hokey Pokey" with "left foot," "right hand," "left hand," "right elbow," "left elbow," "nose," "whole body," etc.

Activity Two: "I have a headache" (_____ache)

Vocabulary for Activity Two

- Know
- Don't
- Look
- Very
- Well
- Okay
- No
- Not
- Really
- What's
- Matter
- Have
- Headache
- Stomachache
- Earache
- _____ache

Dialogue for Activity Two

A. "You don't look very well. Are you feeling okay?"
B. "No, not really."
A. "What's the matter?"
B. "I have a headache." (Practice with other aches too.)
A. "I'm sorry to hear that."

1. **Introduce Vocabulary**
   - Write the words on the board.
   - Review the words with the students.

2. **Model/Comprehension Check**
   - Teacher A: "You don't look very well. Are you feeling okay?"
   - Teacher B: "No, not really."
   - Teacher A: "What's the matter?"
   - Teacher B: "I have a headache." (Practice with other aches too.)
   - Teacher A: "I'm sorry to hear that."

3. Repetition of Dialogue between Teacher and Group:

- Teacher: "You don't look very well. Are you feeling okay?"
- Group: "You don't look very well. Are you feeling okay?"
- Teacher: "No, not really."
- Group: "No, not really."
- Teacher: "What's the matter?"
- Group: "What's the matter?"
- Teacher: "I have a headache." (Practice with other aches.)
- Group: "I have a headache."
- Teacher: "I'm sorry to hear that."
- Group: "I'm sorry to hear that."

Repetition with Response

- Teacher: "You don't look very well. Are you feeling okay?"
- Group: "No, not really."
- Teacher: "What's the matter?"
- Group: "I have a headache." (Practice with other aches.)
- Teacher: "I'm sorry to hear that."

4. Drill

Pantomime

- Pantomime an ailment and see if students in the class can guess what's wrong with you.
- Call on student volunteers to pantomime an ailment. (Give candy to volunteers.) Have other students guess the ailment.

Activity Three: Follow the Doctor's Directions

Vocabulary for Activity Three
- Touch
- Hold
- Breath
- Sit
- Table
- Look
- Ceiling
- Cough
- Lie
- On
- Back
- Say
- Raise
- Turn
- Around

Dialogue for Activity Three

A. "Touch your toes."
B. "My toes?"
A. "Yes."
B. Perform the requested action.

A. "Sit on the table."
B. "The table?"
A. "Yes."
B. Perform the requested action.

A. "Hold your breath."
B. "My breath?"
A. "Yes."
B. Perform the requested action.

Continue dialogue with other requests using the vocabulary words. For example:

"Cough."

"Look at the ceiling."

"Say a-ah."

"Roll up your sleeve."

1. **Introduce Vocabulary**
   - Write the words on the board.
   - Review the words with the students.

2. **Model/Comprehension Check**
   - Teacher B: "Touch your toes."
   - Teacher B: "My toes?"
   - Teacher A: "Yes."
   - Teacher B: Perform the requested action.
   -
   - Teacher A: "Sit on the table."
   - Teacher B: "The table?"
   - Teacher A: "Yes."
   - Teacher B: Perform the requested action.

Continue with other examples

3. **Repetition of Dialogue between Teacher and Group**

   Give directions using vocabulary words.
   - Teacher: "Touch your toes."
   - Group: "My toes?"
   - Teacher: "Yes."
   - Group performs the requested action.

   - Teacher: "Sit on the table."
   - Group: "The table?"
   - Teacher: "Yes."
   - Group performs the requested action.

   - Teacher: "Hold your breath."
   - Group: "My breath?"
   - Teacher: "Yes."
   - Group performs the requested action.

- Continue the dialogue with other requests using the vocabulary words. For example:
  - ▷ "Cough."
  - ▷ "Look at the ceiling."
  - ▷ "Say a-ah."
  - ▷ "Roll up your sleeve."
  - ▷ "Turn around."

4. Drill

"The Doctor Says"

- Play this game like "Simon says."
- Give directions for doing things that a doctor might ask his patients to do.
- When you begin with "the doctor says," the group must do what you say.
- When you don't say, "The doctor says," the group should *not* do what you say.
- Whoever follows the instructions when you don't say "The doctor says" is out of the game.

Activity Four—Connect Today's Lesson to the Sixth Day of Creation

Vocabulary for Activity Four
• Fearfully
• Wonderfully

Dialogue for Activity Four

Verse: "For I am fearfully and wonderfully made" (Psalm 139:14).

1. Introduce Vocabulary

- Write the words on the board.
- Review the words with the students.

2. Model/Comprehension Check

Teacher A: Verse: "For I am fearfully and wonderfully made" (Psalm 139:14).

-

3. Repetition of Dialogue between Teacher and Group

- Teacher: "For I am fearfully and wonderfully made" (Psalm 139:14).
- Group: "For I am fearfully and wonderfully made" (Psalm 139:14).

4. Drill

- Pass out cards with words from the verse on them to six students.
- Have the six students line up at the front of the room and arrange themselves in order.
- Have other students practice the verse.

Optional Activity (If Time and English Level Allows): American Idioms

Today we will look at a few idioms that mention body parts since we have been learning these English words today.

"An Arm and a Leg"

- In addition to "arm" and "leg" meaning our actual arm and leg, the expression is used to mean that something is very expensive. When something is expensive and costs a lot of money, you can say that it costs an arm and a leg!

"He Lost His Head"

- The expression "he lost his head" means that someone was angry and overcome by emotions.

"Pulling Your Leg"

- If someone says that she is pulling your leg, she does not mean she is actually pulling on your leg! It is an expression that means that she is tricking you or playing a joke on you.

Conclusion

- God created us perfectly and completely.
- We are truly fearfully and wonderfully made.
- *Put up the circle for the sixth day of creation.* Here is a picture of Adam and Eve and some of the animals that God created on the sixth day.
- This picture shows that God was not far away. God was there all the time watching over Adam and Eve. He is also here today, all the time watching over us!
- At the end of the sixth day, God looked at all that He had made. For the first time, He said that what He had made was not just good; it was *very* good! The day was over, and creation was complete. The Bible tells us, "So the evening and the morning were the sixth day." (Genesis 1:31B)
- *Close the lesson with a prayer thanking God for this day.*

English Lesson Seven

Theme: Creation Day Seven—God Rested!

Materials Needed

- 8-½-by-11-inch copy paper (three pieces per student to fold and make book)
- Stapler and staples
- Color pencils
- Pencil sharpeners
- Re-sealable plastic baggies
- EvangeCubes˚ (or other evangelistic visual tool)
- Flannel board with creation story

Objectives

At the end of lesson seven, students will:

- Recite the memory verses from the previous six days.
- Discuss what God did on the seventh day of creation.
- Discuss the fall of humanity (sin) and what God did for humankind through Jesus.
- Complete a memory book of the week's activities to keep at home.

Introduction:

- Finally, God had completed the work that He started out to do! The Bible says, "Then God blessed the seventh day and sanctified it, because in it He rested from all His work which God had created and made" (Genesis 2:3).
- God rested to indicate to us that He was finished with His creation. For God not only rested on this day, He blessed it and set it apart

as a special day. He wants us to honor Him by having a day of rest each week.

- Adam and Eve were then living in a beautiful garden! *Add the seventh day of creation circle to the flannel board.* They could enjoy some of the delicious fruit of the garden, and they could walk and talk with God. God told them all about creation and the trees and the animals that were there with them. It must have been a beautiful and peaceful place! It was a place where there was no sadness. There was no sickness or disease, either!

- But it did not always stay like this. You know that in our world today we have great tragedy. Later today, we will tell you what the Bible says happened in the garden, why we have pain and sorrow in the world today, and what God has done to provide us with hope and a future!

- Today, we will rest from learning new vocabulary words too! We'll look at the other days and review the past six lessons.

Flannel board demonstrating the seven completed days of creation.
Photo by Steve Parker

Activity One

Review of Bible Verses

Verse from Day One

- Teacher: "Where did everything come from?"
- Group: "In the beginning God created the heavens and the earth" (Genesis 1:1).

Verse from Day Two

- Teacher: "What did God make on day two?"
- Group: "Sky!"
- Teacher: "What verse reminds us that God created the sky?"
- Group: "The heavens declare the glory of God" (Psalm 19:1).

Verse from Day Three

- Teacher: "What verse did we learn to help us remember the third day of creation?"
- Group: "My help comes from the Lord, who made heaven and earth" (Psalm 121:2).

Verse from Day Four

- Teacher: "What verse helps us remember that God made the day and the night?"
- Group: "The day is Yours, the night also is Yours; You have prepared the light and the sun" (Psalm 74:16).

Verse from Day Five

- Teacher: "God made the birds and the fish. He wants us to follow Him and make us fishers of men."
- Group: "Follow Me, and I will make you fishers of men" (Matthew 4:19).

Verse from Day Six

- Teacher: "God made the animals and man and woman."
- Group: "For I am fearfully and wonderfully made" (Psalm 139:1).

Review of Creation Days

- Day one—light
- Day two—sky
- Day three—earth, seas, grass, plants, and fruit
- Day four—sun, moon, and stars
- Day five—birds and fish
- Day six—animals and human beings

We are going have each one of you make a book so that you can remember the days of creation after we are gone! (Use completed book for demonstration.) Let's get going!

Drill

- Divide class into small groups and provide each student with paper for books.
- Demonstrate paper folding to make a book with a page for each day of creation or, alternatively, your team can make blank books ahead of time and pass them out to the students to complete. (See appendix B for instructions on making book.)
- Provide each group with color pencils, sharpeners, and re-sealable baggies after books are made.
- Have students first write on the "tabs" of the book: Day 1, Day 2, etc.
- Allow time for drawing depictions of each day.

Class working on memory book craft project.
Photo by Steve Parker

Activity Two

Review Songs from the Week

A. "This is the Day"
B. "Alleluia—Praise ye the Lord"
C. "Hokey Pokey"
D. "Head, Shoulders, Knees, and Toes"

Activity Three

- At this point, tell the class how sin came into the world and how God sent His son to make provision for our sins. Any evangelism tool can be used, but we chose to use a tool called the EvangeCube˙, which can be purchased prior to the trip at most Christian bookstores or ordered online from the following web site: www.e3resources.org
- We were fortunate to have a Christian translator working with us all week, so we decided to let her present the plan of salvation at this point in the lessons instead of having her translate our words. We purchased one large EvangeCube˙ and a number of small EvangeCubes˙ to pass around the room to the students so that they could follow along while the translator told the story.

Translator sharing the gospel story using the EvangeCube˙.
Picture by Cheryl Parker

Story of Sin and Salvation

- Tell the story of the garden of Eden and sin coming into the world.
- Divide into groups and give each group an EvangeCube.
- Review.

The following outline is taken from the Evangecube© brochure: [1]

"1. Show "Man in Sin" separated from God.

- This light (point to the right side) represents God.
- God is perfect and without sin.
- God loves us!
- God doesn't want us to perish but to have everlasting life.
- But our sins must be removed in order to have eternal life with God.
- This figure (point to the left side) represents every person like you and me.
- The darkness represents our sin.
- Sin is anything that God tells us not to do.
- The Bible says, "All have sinned and fall short of the glory of God" (Romans 3:23).
- Our sins separate us from God.

2. Open to "Christ on the Cross."

- God loved us so much that He sent His only Son Jesus Christ to earth as a man.
- God made Jesus die on a cross to pay for our sins with His blood. He took our sins in His body on the cross so that we could come to God (1 Peter 2:24; 3:18).
- The Bible also says, "God so loved the world that He gave His one and only Son (Jesus) that whoever believes in Him shall not perish but have everlasting life" (John 3:16).
- The Bible says, "God demonstrates His own love for us, in that while we were still sinners, Christ died for us" (Romans 5:8).

3. Open to the "Tomb."

- Men buried Jesus in a tomb.
- They rolled a huge stone in front of it.
- Soldiers guarded the tomb.

4. **Open to "Risen Christ."**

   - God sent an angel to roll away the big stone and scare off the soldiers.
   - God raised Jesus from the dead!
   - Soon afterward, God took Jesus back to heaven.
   - Jesus has paid the price for our sin, and Jesus has conquered death.

5. **Open to "Cross Bridge."**

   - Jesus is the *only way* we can come to God.
   - Jesus said in the Bible, "I am the way, and the truth and the life; no one comes to the Father [God] except through Me" (John 14:6).
   - Through Jesus, we can be forgiven of all our sins and be with God forever.
   - *But just* knowing *about these things is not enough!* We must choose to put our *faith* in Jesus—to *trust* Him to save us from sin.
   - If you do *not* take the *step* of trusting in Jesus, then your sins are *not* removed (Hebrews 4:2).

6. **Open to "Heaven and Hell."**

   - The Bible says that whoever believes in Jesus has *eternal life* and is not judged. But whoever does not believe in Jesus has been judged already, and the *wrath of God* remains upon him (John 3:16, 18, 36).
   - The penalty for sin is death, but eternal life through Jesus is a free gift from God.
   - *What choice will* you *make?*
     - Trust Jesus Christ to be forgiven and have eternal life? (Point to "heaven.")
     - Or reject Jesus Christ and suffer eternal punishment in fire? (Point to "hell.")
   - Would you like to trust Jesus right now and be saved?
   - If Yes:
     - The Bible says, "If you confess with your mouth that Jesus is Lord and believe in your heart that God raised Him from the dead you shall be saved" (Romans 10:9).

- I can lead us in a prayer to God. Remember, it is not saying the words that saves you; God is looking at your *heart* for *true faith in Jesus.* Ready? Let's pray.
- "God, thank you for loving me.
  I confess that I have sinned against You.
  I believe that your son Jesus
  died on a cross
  to pay for my sins and that You raised Jesus from the dead.
  I now put my faith only in Jesus
  to forgive me
  and save me from my sins.
  I confess that Jesus is Lord!
  Thank you for your gift of eternal life.
  I pray in Jesus' name,
  amen."

Assurance of Salvation

1. **Show "Heaven and Hell."**

- If you took that step of trusting in Jesus Christ today, here's what the Bible says about you: "As many as received Jesus, to all who believed in His name, to them He gave the right to become children of God" (John 1:12).
- (Point at the hands.) Jesus also says, "My sheep hear my voice and I know them and they follow Me; and I give eternal life to them and they shall never perish; and no one shall snatch them out of My hand" (John 10:27–28).

2. **Optional step: show "Cross Bridge."**

- Jesus also said, "Whoever hears My word and believes God who sent Me has eternal life and will not be condemned; he has crossed over from death to life" (John 5:24). (Move your finger up the "Cross Bridge" into the light to indicate "crossing over from death to life.") "

  1. *For more information regarding leading someone to Jesus Christ using the Evangecube Puzzle please consult Evangecube's brochure "Unfolding the Answer to Life's Greatest Puzzle" E3 Resources, 317 Main Street, Franklin, Tennessee 37064; (615) 791-7895.*

Conclusion

- Let's end today's lesson by praising God for all that He has done for us and, once again, singing! *Lead class in singing "Alleluia, Praise Ye the Lord."*
- If you accepted Jesus today as your Savior, let us know. We will help you meet other students and adults who know Christ as their personal Savior also so that you can learn more about Him.

Talking to a student about Christ.
Photo by Steve Parker

Appendix A
English Lesson Materials Needed

Lesson One

- World map
- Flannel cloth and board
- Felt "creation" story with piece of black flannel
- "World" beach ball
- Chalk and eraser or dry-erase markers
- Candy, stickers, small toys, pens, and/or pencils
- 8½-by-11-inch card stock to write Bible verse words
- Black marker

Lesson Two

- Flannel board with creation circle for day two
- Prizes for review students
- Toy airplane
- Paper to make paper airplanes
- Crayons to color airplanes
- Pictures representing the prepositions
- Poster paper and markers
- Candy, stickers, pencils, pens, and/or small toys
- 8½-by-11-inch card stock to write Bible verse words

Lesson Three

- Fruit or pictures of fruit
- Vegetables or pictures of vegetables
- Grocery sacks
- "Bingo" cards and markers
- Candy, pencils, pens, small toys, and/or stickers
- Flannel board and day three circle

Lesson Four

- Calendars
- Calendar quiz sheet
- Candy, pencils, pens, small toys, and/or stickers
- Word puzzle game
- Pencils or pens for game
- Cards for the verse (8½-by-11-inch card stock paper and black markers)
- Flannel board and day four creation circle

Lesson Five

- Flannel board with creation circle for day five
- Pictures of fish and chicken
- Concentration cards (three packs)
- 8½-by-11-inch card stock and black markers for verse word cards
- Boxes with pictures for "spin the bottle"
- Candy, pencils, pens, small toys, and/or stickers
- Empty soft drink bottle for "spin the bottle"

Lesson Six

- Flannel board with creation day six circle
- Candy, pencils, pens, small toys, and/or stickers
- 8½-by-11-inch card stock and black marker for verse word cards
- Markers and poster board

Lesson Seven

- 8½-by-11-inch copy paper (three pieces per student to fold and make book)
- Stapler and staples
- Color pencils
- Pencil Sharpeners
- Re-sealable plastic baggies
- EvangeCubes˚ (or other evangelistic visual tools)
- Flannel board with creation story

Appendix B

Listed below are a few of the Web sites and other instructions that can be used for making the games included in the lessons. There are many other sites you can find if you do an internet search, but I hope these will help get you started when preparing for your trip!

World Globe "Beach Ball"

This can be purchased from Operation Mobilization. Their web address is www.usa.om.org.

Making "Bingo" Cards

http://www.teach-nology.com/web_tools/materials/bingo/5/ www.print-bingo.com/print-bingo-cards.php www.dltk-cards.com/bingo

Making Word Search Puzzles

http://www.armoredpenguin.com/wordsearch/ www.puzzles.ca/wordsearch.html

Making the Calendar Quiz

http://www.english-zone.com/grammar/calendar2.html http://www.enchantedlearning.com/subjects/time/quiz/

Making the Concentration Game

- Type eighteen words on paper, spacing them apart so that each one will be the size of a playing card when cut apart.
- Print two copies of the words that you have typed for a total of thirty-six words.
- Laminate the paper and cut the words apart into cards for a total of thirty-six cards.

- To play the game, shuffle and lay out the cards in six rows with six cards in a row.
- Turn over two cards to try to get a match. If there is no match, turn both cards back over and continue with the next player until all players are able to match cards.

Making Memory Books (Day Seven)

- Take three pieces of 8-½-by-11-inch copy paper for each book that you want to make.
- Fold the first piece of paper on the 8-½-inch edge so that there is 4-inch flap.
- Fold the second piece of paper on the 8-½-inch edge so that there is a 4-½-inch flap.
- Fold the third piece of paper on the 8-½-inch edge so that there is a 5-inch flap.
- Insert the third piece into the second, and then fold those two into the first.
- Staple on the folded edge. You will have a handmade booklet that will have six tabs: one for each day of creation.
- Students can then label each tab Day 1 through Day 6. They can decorate each page according to what God made on that day. This will be a take home craft project that will remind them of these lessons long after you are gone!

Final Note

I would love to hear your stories and experiences using these lessons. You can e-mail me at scparker19@yahoo.com.

LaVergne, TN USA
08 April 2011
223438LV00002B/5/P